In

The

Right

Direction

A Beginner's Guide To Starting A Record Label

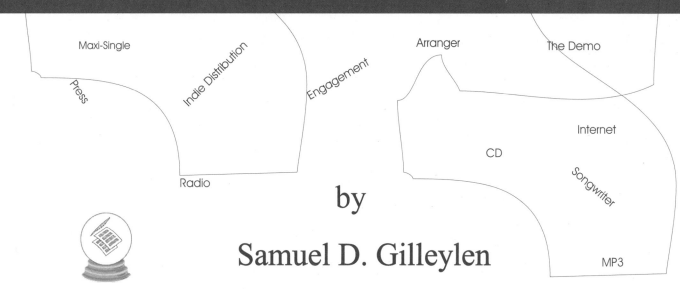

by

Samuel D. Gilleylen

Future Mix Publications
Memphis, TN

3rd Edition

Dedication

This Edition is dedicated to my lovely wife, Joyce Gilleylen.

Gilleylen, Samuel D.

IN THE RIGHT DIRECTION - A Beginner's Guide To Starting A Record Label

(3rd Edition)

ISBN 0-9723042-0-7

Library of Congress Catalog Number: 2002093492

SAN 254-7708

Published by Future Mix Publications, P.O. Box 181356, Memphis, TN 38181

Book Cover and Logo by: **MusicGraphics**

For more publications by Samuel D. Gilleylen visit our website at:

www.FutureMix.biz

Introduction

A famous jazz musician once gave a seminar at a college that I was attending. The aging musician said "You guys have it very easy, because everything that you're interested in learning, in this day and time, is written down for you in books. All you have to do is to get the books and read. When I was a young man we had to invent or learn through trial and error, which took us longer to learn our craft."

Hearing him say this struck a nerve in me because the library had always been one of my favorite places since childhood. I'd always done some type of research in the library either on subjects that no one seemed to have the right answers to or on subjects that no one seemed to be interested in, but me.

Being a songwriter, musician and arranger I have sent out numerous demos (over the years) to record companies' A&R departments. If I'd known then what I know today, I would have invested the money that I paid recording studios (and the post office) toward my own independent label.

The recording industry is a jungle full of hungry animals always craving a sucker for dinner. Learn as much as you can to protect yourself. Reading books and magazines on the recording industry and the music business will help you to survive and achieve your foothold (and share of profits) in this business.

Thank you for purchasing this book. Evidently you are very interested in forming your own record label. For a little more than the price of a CD you have purchased knowledge that will pay for itself many times over.

You have taken your first step in the right direction.

Another word from the author

"All of the books that I read, when I was trying to do research about the biz, were thick and the information that I received from these books was (at the time) way over my head. There was information about all of these contracts and organizations, when all I wanted to do was to release my own record. I was already my own music producer, arranger, publisher and label. I felt that I was doing a lot of reading that didn't even pertain to my situation.

I was more concerned with how to get radio air play, how to distribute and sell my records, how to promote my record and how to set up engagements for myself in hopes of attracting a major label. I was trying to do an independent release! As I became more involved with the industry I began to realize that there weren't too many books on the market for those who were trying to start their own labels. Most of the books on the market were gear toward bands that were already touring or professional people who were already out there actively gigging and looking toward a major record deal.

After I formed my independent label, Jamsmith Records in 1986 and released a single on myself (Quadrant-U), I began to think more and more about one day writing a book for those who are trying to break into the independent record industry. Thus the ideal for... "IN THE RIGHT DIRECTION - A Beginner's Guide To Starting A Record Label" was born.

I have tried to cover most of the things that I've had to deal with over my years in the business. In doing so I have designed sort of a road map for those who have little or no experience in the biz, but who desire to start their own independent record label. A lot of successful independent modern rockers and rap artists have taken this approach! I hope that my book will benefit all who care to purchase and to read it. "

Sincerely,

Samuel D. Gilleylen
    (Author)

Table of Contents

****Plus 4 Bonus Pages*****

Trademark
Taxation
Start-up Check List
Demos & Releases

Chapter 1

Do You Have A Commercial Product?

Listening To Radio

Most undiscovered recording artists have the same idea, and that is to be original. This is a good thought, but on the journey towards achieving this they take it to the extreme. This then results in the product sounding weird.

Some years ago, I was an independent recording artist with the same ideal. I recorded a song that I thought would change the music industry. Since I was a versatile musician who could play a variety of instruments (and styles), I totally disregarded the styles that were popular on the radio. I made my single dance, rock, and everything in-between.

Thus, I ended up with this strange song that didn't have a strong style, so therefore no radio station would play it. The song had no format. Urban radio stations said that it was Rock and Roll, the Rock stations said that it was Pop, etc. Radio stations are not going to disappoint their listening audiences by playing a song that doesn't fit their play list format.

For example: If you were listening to a Hip-Hop or Pop station and the DJ played a slow Jazz or classical song you would probably change the dial, ... right? I know I would.

You don't have the money for heavy promotions and advertising (like some of the famous weird sounding superstar artists that are currently selling a multi-platinum product). You should listen to a radio station that plays your favorite style of music. Model your music after what a station's listening audience likes to hear, and you can't go wrong. A new artist has to build a strong following within a certain format to be successful or to be able to crossover. **Madonna** and **Michael Jackson** are living proof.

The current radio formats are:

-CHR / Pop
-Hip-Hop / Rap
-Dance/Club
-Rock
-Adult Contemporary / AC
-Christian
-Latin
-Modern Rock / Alternative
-Urban or Rhythm & Blues
-Smooth Jazz
-New Age
-World Music
-Electronic
-Reggae
-Blues
-Gospel
-Country

Standard radio Formats are:

-Black Gold or Vintage Soul
-Vintage Rock & Roll
-Classical or Jazz
-Oldies or Nostalgic
-Talk or News

Radio station formats can be found in both **R&R Magazine** and **Billboard Magazine** at these sites:

www.radioandrecords.com
www.billboard.com

Listening To Hot Producers

Every song and artist has a producer. Some artists produce themselves, but this is not often the case. When you're reading a CD or cassette insert, look for the producer's name. You might find that some of your favorite artists have the same producer. A producer who is <u>hot</u> (a hit maker) in a certain format often produces for different record companies that are releasing artists within his format.

Most producers of today also write and arrange songs for their artists. If you are an aspiring songwriter and arranger, it will be helpful for you to become familiar with the songs and musical arrangement styles of the producers who are producing your favorite artists. Also, since you plan on starting your own record label, you might want to read weekly top 40 retail charts (for your style of music) to find out what most people are buying. Concentrate on the songs that you love which are in the top 10. This way you will know what type of artists and/or songs you might consider releasing.

Listening To Your Worst Critic

Learning to listen to opinions from others is very valuable. If someone (who is into your style of music) says that he doesn't like your song, ask him why? Then ask him what can you do to make it sound better? He might have some information that you can then use to rearrange your song slightly and at the same time give your song the missing ingredients to appeal to hundreds more like him.

Most new labels and artists get very angry when someone says that their song is a piece of crap. As you go on your journey to success, you will learn that in order for your product to be successful it must appeal to a broad audience.

Friends & Family

You've gotta love 'em. However, these people aren't good critics, because they love you. It's a mental thing. Friends and close family members are going to give you encouraging words always. Your song might make dogs howl or put people to sleep. It's best to let people who don't know you hear your sound. Let a stranger listen in the mall, public library over a walkman or in the park over your boom box or car radio. "Hey listen to this new artist, what do you think?"

Listening To Industry People

There are Music Industry Professionals in your local area. These include: Radio Station Program Directors, Nightclub DJs, Tour promoters, Recording Engineers, Music Publishers, and Retail Outlets (Record store buyers). These people know what is hot in all radio formats.

You can put these people into your "worst- of- the- worst critic" list. These people aren't afraid to tell you that your song is trash or if you have a hit on your hands! Also, many times they will offer you constructive advice if you are courteous and ask.

The philosophy of these people is:

"If you are a new artist or legitimate new label you should be professional enough to take criticism as a vehicle to make changes, and to better yourself."

Chapter 2

Establishing Your Business

Upon starting your record label you will need a business name and logo. Of course you have a name or a picture in mind, don't you? Once you decide upon a name, you will need a trademark attorney to do a name search for you. This will assure that no one else is using the same name. Have him assist you in getting a trademark for your name & logo. This way no one can use your name or logo without your permission.

Unless you can draw your own logo, you will need a graphic artist. A graphic artist can take your mental ideal or single word and develop it into professional artwork for a camera ready logo (See your local yellow pages or favorite music magazine) . Camera ready means that this logo can be re-sized by a printer and printed on whatever products you want to put it on. Most print shops have stock logos that everyone can use, but then 100s of other people will wind up using the same logo! Be original let a graphic artist create a logo for you. You can also use this artist later to layout and design your posters and CD or cassette inserts (if you like his work).

Next, you'll need to open a business checking account in your label's name. Inquire at your local bank about this. Banks usually require a minimum of $100.00 to open a business checking account. You should make all of your purchases from here on out with a company check. Studio sessions, musical equipment, CDs, Tapes, Business or Offices supplies, printing, etc. are considered business purchases. Your cancelled checks will be your receipts for taxes.

This will not only make your label look legitimate, but it will also help you keep track of all you expenses to prepare tax information for the IRS. You will need an accountant. A CPA (Certified Public Accountant) will be able to help you in this area if you keep all of your receipts and cancelled checks. The Federal Government requires all businesses to file taxes yearly. Business purchases for each year are usually tax deductible. Your state might require you to have a business license. Ask your CPA about this.

Modern Communications and Technology

Cellular phone technology has really change the way that we communicate in the 21st century. Today's PCS cellular phones not only serves as mobile phones with multiple voice mailboxes, but one can also send and receive faxes, emails, and surf the net ....from just about anywhere in the world!!!! This technology is known as wireless communications.

You now have more options to stay in contact industry professionals. Now those out-of-town record retailers can fax your checks in a matter of minutes (no more "Your check is in the mail").

Another form of modern technology is mobile computing. This include the <u>handheld computers</u> (HPC) and the palm sized computers (the Palm Pilot being the original model). These powerful little computers can store all of your contact information, expense records, appointments, goals, business plans, etc. These wonder toys can do just about anything that a desktop pc can do.... but while you are on the go (in a car, plane, boat, remote beach, hotel room, etc.). Use a portable printer and you can also do your word processing, spreadsheets, invoices, faxing, and fax check printing....anywhere.

Most of these little computers have fast onboard modems which uses a telephone cord and plugs into any telephone wall outlet. *There is also usually a slot on-board these computers to insert a card modem. With the card modem you can plug your cellular phone into these computers and you will be able to send and receive faxes, emails and surf the internet.....from just about anywhere in the world!!!!! There are also cell phones that will allow you to all these things as well!

*Palm sized computers will usually have attachable modems instead of the card modems. For HPC users there is a 1-peice data modem unit that will eliminate the need for one to attach a cell phone for wireless communications (check your retail computer store and your cellular phone service provider for more information about these products).

The Professional Image

If you were running a store, for instance, you would be leery of someone who comes in wearing ragged clothes, talking fast in slang, and looking like he is going to rob you. Well, believe it or not, this is the way that some people who are starting independent record labels conduct themselves.

Since a record label is a business, the more you conduct yourself like a business owner, the more respect you will receive from music industry professionals. Until you reach a certain level of success, communicate properly by using English not slang when talking to industry people. (Slang is okay to use back at your office or in the studio.)

In running a business there are things required to give you that professional image such as:

-Career oriented clothes to wear when meeting with professional people in the field (White Shirt, Tie, dress slacks, sox, dress shoes, Attache, or career oriented clothes for ladies etc.). Try to be always on time or call if you can't make it.

-Renting a P. O. Box for demos and business documents that you will receive.

-Raised print business cards to leave with people that might be of some assistance
 to your career.

-Raised print letterhead and stationery printed with your business logo

-Access to a computer

-Invoices for product that you will have in record stores on consignment

-Voice Mail with a short professional greeting

-Business Card file and/or organizer so that you won't lose contact with the
 connections   that you make

Your local telephone company can add voice mail to your home telephone line for a small monthly fee (also multiple mailboxes and call forwarding to your pager and/or cell phone).

Nowadays anyone can print business cards and stationery with a home computer. This is fine if you are in a <u>pinch</u> (out of raised print cards and stationery) and far better than scratching your name and phone number on a piece of paper! Stationery and cards with raise print shows that your company is professional, especially if you are dealing with large well known companies. A local print shop can assist you with raised print business cards; stationery and letterhead, fax sheets, flyers, posters, stickers or other paper items containing your logo.

Your office is practically waiting for you if you own a home computer. With the proper software, you can print most of your items at home as needed. With a modem card installed in your computer, you could have voice mail with multiple mailboxes, fax machine, database for important contacts and much more!

Stay Current & Know Your Trade

Stay on top of what is happening in the music industry.

Start reading <u>R&R</u> (Radio and Records) magazine. This magazine radio stations' playlists and information by genre of music. This is a valuable info resource for the indie label because it also contains radio stations' contact information including: the names of program directors, phone numbers and addresses.

Record labels also monitor this magazine to see if their songs are <u>in rotation</u> (on a particular radio station's play list), which means that these songs are getting airplay. Other information such as: the Top 30 charts for all genres of music, television music video channels' rotation lists, industry news, <u>concert revenue</u> (how much an artist made at a recent concert) and industry ads is included as well.

A subscription to **Radio and Records** magazine will cost a few hundred dollars annually, but it can also be purchased weekly at major book chains for about $7 per copy. If your label is promoting an artist release it would be ideal for you to stay on top of it's progress.

Billboard magazine will contain cutting edge music industry news, names of the songwriters who wrote the songs that are on the charts for all genres of music, the music publishing company names and <u>affiliation</u> (**ASCAP**, **BMI** or **SESAC**), Top selling CDs and singles (soundscan information), label who released each song, the producer's or production company's name, the distributors....and much more! This magazine is also sold weekly at about $7 per copy.

<u>**CMJ**</u> (College Music Journal) monitors college radio activity...Check it out on the web at: CMJ.com

Attend recording industry seminars and talent shows. You will meet either artists or professional industry people who could possibly provide the information or services that you'll need to get your label up and running. Have plenty of business cards, also collect plenty at these functions. Networking and "who you know" plays a big role in this business. Build your own reference library with the latest music business books on the market.

Start your reference library with these books:

This Business of Music, Eight Edition
by M. William Krasilovsky and Sidney Shemel
*****Includes a CD with ready-to-use contracts!!!***** $29.95

The Complete Guide To Internet Promotion For Musicicans
by John Dawes & Tom Sweeney $29.95

Music Publishing A Songwriters Guide, Revised by Randy Poe $18.99

Copyrights © ‚ A Guide For The Music Industry $16.95
by Songwriter Products Ideas & Necessities

The Dictionary Of Music Business Terms by Tom Whitsett $29.95

Start and Run Your Own Record Label by Daylle Deanna Schwartz $16.95

The Music Business (Explained In Plain English) by David Nagger $12.95

REMEMBER THAT YOU ARE THE CHIEF EXECUTIVE OFFICER OF YOUR RECORD LABEL. YOU
MUST LOOK THE PART, CONDUCT YOURSELF IN A BUSINESS-LIKE MANNER, AND KNOW WHAT'S
GOING ON WITH YOUR LABEL AS WELL AS THE RECORDING INDUSTRY.

Record Label Agreements

You will need <u>agreements</u> (contracts) for recording artists, songwriters, musicians, record producers, club owners or talent buyers, etc. Agreements in the recording industry are just "deals" between two parties. Some of the things that will be negotiated within these agreements are standard practice and other things are special requests agreed upon according to a balance of each company's <u>best interest </u>(to benefit each company equally).

You will need an entertainment attorney to customize your contracts with what your label has and can offer to people. Many new label owners make the mistake of thinking that all recording contracts are the same. If you're not at a millionaire's status why offer your recording artist millions to record your demo?

The Golden Music Industry Rule: Always let an Entertainment Attorney advise you and to negotiate contracts for you.

Why do you need an entertainment attorney and aren't all attorneys created equally? Well ... yes and no. You have to ask yourself or all doctors created equally? Would you go to a medical doctor for a tooth filling? The recording industry changes frequently and entertainment attorneys are always up on the latest trends and contracts that the industry has to offer. Sure, any attorney can read and write contracts, but what is his specialty?

Be sure to mention to your entertainment attorney that your record label plans on doing a variety of things <u>in-house </u>(independently or without the help of outside companies). This way he can customize standard agreements for all areas of your label.

<u>These things will include</u>:

Music publishing
Independent record production
Independent record promotion and distribution
Artist development and management

Other services that your label will need can be paid for as needed.

<u>Some of these things will include</u>:

Graphic Artist / Layout person
Commercial Printing
Accountant Fees
Record Pressing, CD replication or Cassette Duplication
Photography
Recording Studio Rental & Engineer Fees
Attorney Fees (.............of course!)

Chapter 3

Copyrights, Music Publishing, and Royalties

Copyrights

Whenever a songwriter writes a song, he should get it copyrighted. He can copyright this unpublished version of a song with a cassette tape containing only lead vocals & piano (or lead vocals & guitar). To do this he should file a copyright **Form PA**, along with the cassette tape and lyric sheet, with the **Library of Congress Copyright Office in Washington, DC**. A record label should get a few of the following copyright forms: **PA, CA**, and **SR** . These forms are free and can be found at public libraries or by calling the Copyright Office (*See Appendix 1 in the back of this book*). Copyright forms come with submission instructions and the filing fee is currently $30.00 per form.

If the same songwriter writes a group of songs, he can copyright his whole unpublished collection (instead of an individual song) for only $30.00. Let's suppose he has written 5 of 12 songs for your artist's new CD. These first 5-songs can be copyrighted under a "*Collective Name*" with a form PA and the other 7 songs can be copyrighted at a later date when he has finished them. He can give this first group of 5-songs a collective name (such as: *My First Songs*) and file copyright Form PA for a $30.00 fee. Make sure to include the cassette demo tape or CD containing these songs with music and all the lyric sheets. These songs are protected as soon as they are dropped into the mailbox.

The Copyright Office will mail back the Form PA within a few weeks with a copyright number assigned. When the additional 7-songs are finished, he will need to mail another copyright **Form CA**, along with another demo cassette or CD containing the additional 7-songs with lyric sheets. There will be another fee, but he will have copyrighted all 12 of his unpublished songs and paid 2-fees instead of 12.

If you use different songs from several songwriters then each songwriter should file his own PA copyright form. To save yourself legal hassles make sure that your artist records songs that your songwriters have copyrighted and assigned to your <u>publishing wing </u>(your label's publishing company). See your Entertainment Attorney for further details.

Before releasing songs on CDs, tapes, or records, your label should file a copyright **<u>Form SR</u>** (sound recording) to protect your label's recorded version of the songs. This way no one will be able use recorded samples of these songs or it's music tracks without the copyright <u>owner's permission</u> (without compensating him). Rap artists as well as some alternative artists use samples frequently. You must submit (2) finished CDs, cassettes, or records with the copyright Form SR. Afterwards a circle "P" followed by the year and your record label name should be printed on the CD, the CD inserts as well as any printed materials. This represents the year that this recorded version was <u>published</u> (made available for public sell) by your label.

A copyrighted song legally belongs to the writer, whose name appears on the copyright. No one can use or reproduce his song in <u>any manner </u>(Recorded, Written, or in a live performance) without the writer's authorization. This keeps others from making profits from the songwriter's song without the songwriter <u>getting paid </u>(receiving royalties). Afterwards, the songwriter should use his copyright information (such as: © 2002 John Henry) on all the unpublished demo tapes and lyric sheets that he submits to others.

The Publisher and Music Publishing

Recording artists only release published songs. <u>Published</u> means to prepare and issue for public distribution or sale (reproduced on CD, cassette, music video..., etc.). To publish a song, the songwriter will have to assign his song to a music publisher. By signing a <u>Songwriter's and Music Publisher's Agreement</u> (Popular Songwriter's Contract) with a publisher, the Music Publisher then becomes the songwriter's power of attorney. This gives the Publisher the authority to license record labels, film directors, and others to use the songwriter's song on a royalty basis.

The Songwriter's and Music Publisher's Agreement also determines what percentage of the song publishing royalties each party will receive. It is customary for the publisher and the writer to split royalties 50% - 50%.

Example:
Let's say that MICA Records Publishing wing wants to negotiate a deal with the original publisher. The MICA publisher is offering the original publisher a $50,000.00 cash advance + future royalties to use the songwriter's song as a record release on a new artist. Since the original publisher is splitting 50-50 with the writer, the writer will receive $25,000.00 of this cash advance + 50% of all other future royalties that the original publisher will receive.

If the song was a collaboration project, the percentage for each writer and/or arranger should be written within the publisher's agreement. A song consists of both words and music, therefore the arranger will get 1/2 of the writer's 50% share, (25%), because he has supplied the music. (Unless the arranger is a work-for-hire employee and signs an agreement as such with the writer and /or publisher. In this case the arranger will receive a set fee and usually no royalties).

In other words, if the writer and the arranger collaborated on a song then the publisher will get 50%, the writer will get 25%, and the arranger will get 25% of all that song's publishing royalties.

As previously mentioned there is a spot on the Music Publisher's Agreement for collaboration percentages. See Music Publishing A Songwriter's Guide for more detailed information on this.

If a song becomes a hit, a larger publisher will usually want to negotiate with the original publisher for the use of the song. The larger publisher will receive 1/2 of the original publisher's share. This is called a sub-publishing agreement between the two publishers only. In this case the sub-publisher will get 25% of original publisher's share of publishing royalties. Because this deal involves only the two publishers, the writer will still receive his 50% of the original publisher's new share.

<u>Notice that on cassette tape and CD inserts all songwriters' names will usually appear underneath the song titles such as:</u>

I Knew Her Yesterday
If one writer: (M. Smith)

Someday Tonight
If three writers: (M. Smith / T. Brown / D. Ott)

Performing Rights Royalties

There are two types of royalties that a songwriter and publisher can receive. The royalties that the songwriter and publisher receive from a performing-right organization are called Performance royalties. The other royalty, Mechanical Royalties, comes from the actual sell of items containing the published song (CDs, Tapes, records, Videos, sheet music..., etc.). Thus the term "royalties" is used frequently in describing the combination of these (2) forms of royalties.

First we will look at performance royalties.

Performing-Right Organizations such as ASCAP, BMI and SESAC collect a fee each time a song plays in public (US and other countries). A song plays to the public in various forms: radio air play, nightclub play, television ads, music videos, movie soundtracks, live performances by artists, muzak (music that is heard in grocery stores, elevators, airplanes, Exxon....etc.) intercom music systems, as well as jukebox selections. Both the publisher and writer members receive part of these moneys 3-4 times yearly (quarterly). These royalties come in the form of royalty checks which are mailed directly to each member's address. This royalty pays a few cents each time a song is played on the radio......imagine a hit song being played about a few thousand times within a 3-5 month period!

If your label is its own publisher, then you should affiliate with (join) a performing-right organization as a music publisher member. You can choose any name of your choice for your publishing company and pay a small annual fee. If you are a songwriter, then you should also affiliate as a writer member. There is another small annual fee for writer members. If there are other songwriters within your record company, then they should affiliate also (to be able to receive their performing-right royalties). To affiliate with one of these organizations call them for both membership packets (Publisher's and Writer's). Be sure to order enough writer members' packets to have some on hand for future writers whom may join your label (or artists who write their own songs).

If your label (you) is both the writer and the publisher of a published song, then your label will receive two performance royalty checks (One for the writer member and one for the publisher member).

Once affiliated with one of these organizations, you should always include your publisher's name and affiliation within record release credits (which are printed on lyric sheets, demos, CD and cassette tape inserts, etc..). Look at a few cassette tape or CD inserts and see how the publishers and their affiliation information are printed.

Example:

If only one publisher-
        On The Roof (ASCAP)

If two or more publishers (A Sub publishing deal has occurred)-
        On The Roof (ASCAP) / Used Gear (BMI) / Country Boy (SESAC)

Mechanical Royalties

As mentioned above, songwriters and publishers also receive mechanical royalties. This is when a publisher issues a **compulsory mechanical license** to a record label to reproduce and market a song for an artist's release. If your label is handling it's own publishing, then you will simply issue this license from your publishing wing to your label. Your Entertainment attorney can assist with this.

Mechanical Royalties work like this:

1) Once a label arranges distribution with a record store or one-stop, these outlets pay the label with checks for the sale of the label's CDs, tapes, and records.

2) The label pays the publisher with a check for the sale of each product containing the publisher's songs. The current mechanical royalty in which the label pays to a publisher is 8-cents for the sale of each song up to 5-minutes recorded onto CD, Tape, Music Video, 12-inch, Movie Soundtrack, sheet music..., etc.

3) The publisher then pays the songwriter a check for the percentages that were agreed upon in the Songwriter's and Publisher's Agreement. Out of the 100% of the music publishing royalty possible per song which is .08-cents: Both the **Songwriter's share** and the **Publisher's share** is 50% which is .04-cents per each song (up to 5-minutes long that is recorded onto CD, Tape, 12-inch, etc). This .04-cents songwriter's share is then divided between the number of writers, if there are more than one writer. The .04-cent publisher's share is then divided between the number of music publishers, if there are more than one publisher.

It's always a good idea for an <u>indie</u> (independent) label to have as many services in-house as possible. This way they get to keep more of the royalties from the sale of their products. Most indie labels have their own songwriters, arrangers, musicians and music publisher. Most indie labels have their own recording studios and engineers as well.

If your label will have it's own in house functions then **<u>Mechanical Royalties</u>** (monies from record sales) must be recorded and accounted for. These monies must then be divided and distributed between the label, publisher, songwriters, producers and the artists. Your accountant can do this for you, as well as prepare everyone's royalty statement.

(*Again, all this information is in* **Music Publishing a Songwriter's Guide** *and* **The Musician's Business and Legal Guide**.) *Check your local bookstore and buy the most recent editions.*

Artist and Producer Royalties

A new independent recording artist royalties are usually start at 8% of 90% the label's net profit from sells of album length CDs, Tapes or Vinyl and 4% of 90% of the label's net profit from sells of singles and maxi-singles CDs Tapes or Vinyl sold in the USA. Artist royalties are 1/2 the above percentages for foreign country sells. The producer's royalty is usually around 3% of the label's net profit of CDs Tapes or Vinyl sold. The first 10% of the label's net profits go toward the packaging and artwork of the release. The producer is usually paid out of the artist's royalties even though the record label will in most cases pay the producer and charge it to the artist as an advance against the artist's royalties. A recording artist won't be eligible for any royalties from record and CD sells, until the record label has <u>recouped</u> (made back) all of the money that has been spent on the artist's initial release. (See page 55 for more on this subject).

Chapter 4

Recording In The 90s and Beyond

If you're not releasing a <u>self-contained recording artist </u>(one who write and sing songs, arrange, play his / her own music tracks in the recording studio) then you will have to have a recording artist and a producer. 90's home recording studios (as well as most indie studios today) contained: MIDI keyboard workstations, samplers, advanced compact mixers, digital multi-track recorders, DAT machines, audio cassette and CD recorders. It is now possible to record professional masters at home!

The current trend in the recording industry is the use of computers. The software used for professional music production will range from synthesizer sequencing, rhythm or drum programming, sampling, digital multi-track recording and mastering. Again.....it is now possible to compose, record and master your own CD with a home computer!!! This super software can be found in your local musical instrument stores and in magazines such as **Electronic Musician**, **Keyboard**, **Mix**, etc... **Pro Tools** is currently one of the hottest software packages for computer.

Most of the Pop and Hip-hop hits that are recorded today have been through the use of one of the above technologies .....a lot of dance remixes!!!

Independent Producers

Producers a few years ago had to employ the services of many people to record a song master for a record release. These producers had to hire a songwriter, an arranger, a professional band of musicians, background vocalists, and professional recording engineers. Recording a record was not only expensive, but try dealing with attitudes or problems of these many people.

With the invention of MIDI (Musical Instrument Digital Interface) synthesizer workstations, samplers, and digital recording equipment, producers of today are self-contained. Today's producers are musicians and/or midi programmers. Today's indie producers can also write and arrange songs. They can compose and perform professional music tracks to songs. With the use of samplers, they can sing and record background vocals to their own lead vocals, and engineer the whole session in their bedroom! Then, take the masters to a pressing company for CD replication. The age of the self-contained producer is upon us.

This type of person is an asset to an indie record label, especially if the producer is also the artist! You have only one person to deal with or to pay royalties to! If you are fortunate enough to be the label and this producer. Guess what? You make and keep all the royalties. Surprise!...most indie label owners are producers who have started a label to release themselves and later find vocalists to produce as artists for their label. One such producer is known as **Babyface**.

If you are starting a record label, you are probably one of these producers yourself. If you are not one of these producers, then this is the type of producer whom you should be looking for. You can find this type of producer in musical instrument stores looking at new synthesizers, samplers or digital recording equipment. Music store salespeople know these people well. Some music store sales people are producers who sell musical equipment as a day job (they play in a band or in a studio during their off time). You might want to visit a music store to tell one of these salespeople that you are starting a new label and you are searching for a producer. Be sure to leave them your business card and tell them the type of music that you plan on releasing.

<u>Also you can:</u>

Advertise in local or regional newspapers, music papers, and Radio Stations (If your budget allows this). Have those who inquire send demos to your P. O. Box. That way you can call the producer of your choice.

Visit University Music Departments and leave flyers on the bulletin boards.
Some record stores might let you leave flyers near their Top 40 lists.
Call or visit Recording Studios. If you visit, always leave your business card.

Screening A Producer

If you like a demo that you've received from a producer, call this person and ask these questions:

-What can you do? (Get his list of skills)
-Did you do everything on this demo?
-Do you want to be an artist or a producer?
-Are you a songwriter and did you write the lyrics? Is that you singing?
-Do you have more songs that we can hear?
-Do you know singers whom you'd like to produce that we could audition for a possible
  recording contract?

Most producers desire to be artists. If you can find one who is easy to work with, then you are on your way to establishing your label quickly.

If your producer is <u>self-contained</u> (does everything) you will need an **Independent Record Producer's Agreement**, a **Recording Artist Agreement**, and a **Songwriter's and Publisher's Agreement**. Have your entertainment attorney advise you and negotiate these for you with your producer.

*AS MENTIONED ABOVE YOU WILL ONLY HAVE TO PAY ROYALTIES TO ONE PERSON... **if that person is your artist, your songwriter, and your producer.**

Independent Recording Artists

You will want to deal with recording artists who are <u>independent</u> (meaning that they have not signed contracts with any other party). Warning!!!!! Recording artists can be very temperamental people with many hang-ups. You have girls whose boyfriends might not want them to come to the studio sessions or guys who have to choose between "the woman" or the recording session on every other occasion. Then there are those singers who don't write songs, but hate every song that your songwriter comes up with (or hate all the musical arrangements that the producer arranges). Some have severe ego problems, the classic *"I'm a star already"* mentality.

When choosing a recording artist, you must carefully screen them. Have them to submit a <u>Press kit</u> (cassette demo or CD package with photo, bio, along their phone number) and <u>SASE</u> (self addressed stamped envelope) to your P. O. Box. This way you can return their packet if you don't like what you hear, and they won't know how to call or where to find you (to keep bugging you about recording them). If an aspiring artist hasn't taken the time to record some type of demo or isn't willing to take the time, then they aren't very serious about a career.

Listen to a demo and if you like what you hear, then you can call the singer. Chat with the singer and find out what she is like mentally. You shouldn't get involved with her if all this singer can talk about is money and her likes and dislikes. This person isn't serious and wants to be in the business for the wrong reasons. This type of artist will be very hard to work with.

A true singer wants to be an artist because that's what she likes to do. She knows that the money and fame will come with success. If she talks about loving to entertain people or delivering a message to people through a song, then you have a potentially good artist. The singer thinks like an artist, therefore she will put her all into any song. She understands that you are just starting you label and might not be able to offer her what a major label can offer. Anything that you have to offer her to better her career she's willing to try. She will be humble and work well with people that you assign to her. This is the type of person that you should call in for an interview and audition. This singer will make a great artist.

If you plan on dealing with child singers (Minors), then you will want your entertainment attorney to advise you and to negotiate **a parental permission agreement** with the minors' parents.

If you like what you hear then give the artist an interview phone call:
-Have you signed any contracts with anybody?
-Are you of legal age?
-Ask them why this business?
-Inquire about how much they know about the business?
-Ask them what they expect from your label?
-Tell them what your label has to offer and have them come and audition for you (If Interested).

Artist Image

Artist image and stage presence are what make a recording artist more than just a singer. Every recording artist has an image. Be it bad boy, gentleman, lady, bad girl, etc. Artist image is just as important as the format of music that the artist will be singing.

In creating an artist image for your artist you have to be concerned with (3) major things:

1) **The artist's personality**. Listen to the types of songs that the artist sounds best on. Is this particular style shy, serious, playful, sexy, etc. What is it about this artist's way of singing that makes you want to sign him or her? Build upon that.

2) **Visual appearance**. What types of clothing does this artist look best wearing? What looks natural on this person? What does the artist feel best wearing? What hair styles and/or make-up does this person look best in?

3) **What major artist does your artist remind you of**? What artists does your artist idolize? Build confidence in your artist by letting him or her try to portray all of their idols. The trick is that your artist will eventually wind up with an original style that will be very commercial. They will only copy the things that they like about various artists and combine these into their own style, thus still sounding original, comfortable and confident.

The image you decide upon for your artist has to be something that the artist is comfortable and natural with. Either the song deliverance or the visual appearance will suffer if you try to force an image on an artist. The radio listeners or the audience will know that something isn't right.

Some artists have images already. These people have lived the life of the things that are subjects in the songs that they write or types of songs that they like to sing.

The Photo Shoot

Choose a photographer who is known around town for doing photography on models or bands. These photographers can be found in local music newspaper/magazine ads, or at your daily newspaper's company (*see the entertainment section of your newspaper that have pictures of a local concert*). Call local modeling agencies and inquire about a local photographer who does work for them. The going rate starts at about $100.00 per session. you'll only need one session.

Just as you would use an entertainment attorney for your contract negotiations in this business, you should use a photographer who is experienced in photographing bands or models. There is a big difference in family photos and photos that you see on CD inserts, or on modeling magazines' pages.

Your artist will receive several poses. These pictures can then be used on different products such as posters, 8x10 promotional photos, as well as on the CD inserts. Keep in mind that these photos are what you are using to market your artist to the recording industry. Therefore you'll want your photos to look just as good as the major labels' artists' photos. These photos must capture your artist's image and appeal to your target audience. 8x10 Black & White photos are the standard in this industry. Most magazines and newspapers prefer these to color, unless you're already selling platinum CDs.

Setting A Release Date

All record labels set a release date for new releases. A release date is important in that it gives everyone involved a time frame in which to put all of their resources together to effectively market a new product. You'll need time for studio sessions in order to make master recordings for your new releases. the printer will need a few weeks to layout and print your printed items (CD and cassette inserts, posters, press release materials, etc.). Then add three more weeks for the duplication plant to make your CDs, tapes or vinyl.

After receiving your printed and duplicated product, you will need time to make the following industry contacts:

Most major music magazines need to have ads, press releases, and/or new release CD copies 3-4 months before the actual release date. These magazines receive so many new artist releases that it might take close to a month or two for them to even get a chance to look at and to review your package. Local magazines might need less time, but call them to be sure.

Record store owners or potential record distributors need to receive copies 2-3 months in advance, so they will have time to decide if they want to carry your products. These people also receive hundreds of new releases per month. *ALSO SEE INDEPENDENT DISTRIBUTION- Chapter 6 in this book.*

Radio stations receive literally hundreds of new releases per month for review. Therefore you will need to submit your promotion CD and materials at lease 4-6 weeks before your release date. If your artist will be performing in nightclubs, then you will need about the same time to mail these to nightclub owners for their DJs. *ALSO SEE LOCAL STATIONS- Chapter 6 in this book.*

You will need time to plan your **release party** (party to announce the public of your new release) and to send invitations to industry people. A good time for setting a release date would be the next season after studio master sessions. If you are cutting in the studio in the spring, then pick a day during summer for your release date.

Chapter 5

Record Label Product

The Song Masters

Without songs there would be no artists, no records, and no record labels. Songs are the record labels' most important commodities. A label can function when songs (Hopefully hits) are written, arranged, produced, recorded, and made into product. This product will then be heard and sold to the public for a profit.

On many songs, the songwriter has collaborated (worked jointly) with others to come up with the final lyrics that will be recorded by a recording artist. These other people are most likely other writers, the artist, the producer/arranger, or even the recording engineer. This is standard practice by most record labels. Sometimes, during a recording session, someone might re-write portions of the song or write new parts to make the song sound more commercial (Sound like a style of song on the radio that people would like to buy).

Keep in mind that everyone who participates in coming up with lyrics to a song will have to be paid a percentage of the songwriter's royalties if your label releases the song on an artist. Also, these people should be compensated if the song is performed or broadcasted to the public.

Therefore, a **Songwriter's and Music Publisher's Agreement** should be signed with a percentage beside the name of each person who collaborated on this song. Now each person will be classified as a writer and will receive his share of mechanical royalties from record sales. These writers should also affiliate with a Performing-Right organization (ASCAP, BMI, or SESAC) as writer members so that they will receive performance royalties also when this song is performed or broadcasted to the public. AS MENTIONED IN CHAPTER 3 OF THIS BOOK, ALSO READ THE BOOK, "*MUSIC PUBLISHING A SONGWRITER'S GUIDE*" by RANDY POE.

Consult with your entertainment attorney to see if you have left out any agreements that should be signed before starting each release project.

Once you have found and signed your artist, songwriters and producer/arranger to their appropriate agreements, here are your next (3) steps:

1) Your producer/arranger should work with the writers to arrange and produce enough tracks (recorded musical instrumental arrangements) for a new artist CD (10- 15 songs).

2) Your artist should then rehearse with the writers and learn to sing the lyrics (words) along to the producer's music tracks until songs are perfect. The ideal artist should be able to sing 3-part harmony on other tracks along with his/her own lead vocal track in the studio. Some producers as well as songwriters can sing background vocal tracks in the studio to give songs strong vocal parts.

3) The song demos (demonstration tapes) should be recorded in a recording studio. These tapes will be listened to by you, the producer and others who are involved in the release project for the purpose of having critique sessions. These sessions are important in determining if the recording sounds commercial enough to make master recordings. Sometimes instruments or the artist are out-of-tune, out of rhythm, the tape could have recorded terrible sounding noise, etc.. With these things in mind, it is good to make several demo recordings of a song in order to make it perfect before making the master recording.

ALWAYS copyright your song immediately before anyone takes a copy from the studio, unless you want to take the chance of someone else profiting from it without your permission! Without a copyright, you have no legal proof that the song belongs to your writers or your label.

-REFER TO CHAPTER 3 OF THIS BOOK-

Once studio demos are perfected and are <u>sounding commercial </u>(sounding like songs that are heard on the radio), start recording song masters. Song master recordings (or just.... Masters) are the final studio recordings which are sent out on a <u>DAT</u> (digital audio tape) or a CD master used to make packaged CDs, cassette tapes, or vinyl records...yes, for those who still like to scratch on turntables.

Most people who are new to the recording industry think that you will need a 24-track studio (at $75.00 - $300.00 per hour) to record a professional sounding commercial record release! Well 10 -15 years ago this was true! Again, midi workstation synthesizers, samplers and digital recorders have changed things. Today the quality of home studios that producers use to produce demos may be good enough to use for recording your label's song masters. Especially if he has studio engineering skills, uses all midi instruments and owns digital recording equipment.

If you have been doing your homework and listening to the radio <u>format </u>(music style) that you plan on pursuing, then you should be in tune to that certain format. If the producers' demos sound commercial to you, then release them! If they don't sound quite strong enough then you might want to use a professional engineer and the 24-track studio. Keep in mind that you are on the clock when you go to a 24-track studio. This is not the place for rehearsal unless you have an extensive budget. All music productions/arrangements and vocal parts should be perfect when you go into the 24-track studio.

Bar Code and Record Number

Nearly all the products that are sold in retail stores (especially chain outlets) have Universal Product Codes (UPC or bar codes). Scanner type computer cash registers are becoming the standard in retail outlets. This type of technology allow the managers to see various reports with the push of a computer button. Fast reports such as Inventory (how many of a certain product is left in stock and Sales Tracking (how many have been sold), could save you money if you were calling stores long distance.

Besides being helpful to the retailer, having a UPC on your product gives the impression of the professionalism of your company. Most retailers will ask you if your product has a bar code on it before accepting it for retail. Also if you have a barcode major labels can also track your success through record stores' **SoundScan** reports that are also generated from your CDs sells (when your CD's bar code is scanned at the check-out counter)! *Contact* **SoundScan** *at (914) 684-5525 to order their forms and information package.*

You can now register for a bar code number online (*See Appendix 1 at the back of this book for more info*) and your bar code will be delivered to you by UPS in about 2-weeks.

To register by mail for a UPC, you must contact the Uniform Code Council for an application and information package. There is a one time fee of about $750, however this number can be altered to be used on all of your future products.....FOR THE LIFE OF YOUR COMPANY! The information that you will receive with your number will instruct you how to do this. Once you receive your assigned bar code number, your will configure your bar codes and take these to your graphic artist. The graphic artist can make the actual bar code film for your printer to make different bar codes for printing CD inserts or anything else that your label will market.

When calling the code council, be sure to mention to the council that you will be using this number for a record company. There is special information and digits that are assigned for the recording industry to use on CDs and vinyl. Guess what? You will use bar code numbers as record numbers on all of recorded items' inserts (CDs and records).

Can't afford a bar code right now? **www.discmakers.com** is offering free bar codes if you order your cds from them!!!

Look at the bar codes and record numbers on some of the major artists' cds, cassettes, and singles. You will notice that the record numbers are part of the bar codes. The record number consist of the record label's abbreviation (usually no more than 3 letters) followed by part of the bar code number.

>   Example:
>   Get the new CD of the "Warehouse Men"...on USED GEAR RECORDS.
>   Record Number: UGR12004

Pressing Plants

Labels send song masters which are recorded onto a <u>digital audio tape</u> (DAT) or a reel of tape to record pressing companies (now called tape duplication and CD replication houses). These houses also offer sound processing services (at an additional charge, of course) which enables them to <u>sweeten</u> (add effects such as various reverbs, compression, and other things) to master recordings, which make some recordings sound more professional. However, most of today's producers own elaborate home recording studios where master recordings can be made digitally. Usually, digital masters will need little or no sound processing from the dup house people.

To save money and to see how your finished product will look, all printed items should be typeset and laid out with your recording artist's pictures, label logos, song names, etc., by your graphic artist (CD face art and text, CD inserts and tray-cards, and 12-inch label layouts for vinyl records).The graphic artist can show you a <u>proof</u> (a printed sample) of what your finished products will look like and also make film that the pressing plant can use for professional printing of all your items. The graphic artist might also supply the pressing plant's printer with a professional computer diskette with all of the above jobs laid out exactly the way that you want the finished product to look.

Once you have your song masters in hand (either a DAT or a reel of audio tape), and artwork film or diskette from your graphic artist, the next step is to have the CDs, Cassettes, or vinyl records made. If you are fortunate enough to live in Nashville, L. A., New York, or Atlanta, then you can just drive to the pressing plants. Your product will be ready for pickup within a few days after you drop them off (depending on whom you know)! However, if you are like most of us, you will have to send your master out-of-town and wait 4-8 weeks.

To find a pressing plant, just look into a recent copy of Billboard Magazine (in the classified section). Call some of these places tell them to fax you their rates. Call your local Kinko's to get a fax number and have it faxed there for your pickup (if you don't have a fax machine). Compare prices and services. Call to see how prompt or courteous they are. If you get bad service from a company by phone, then consider using another company.

Since the radio stations play singles, not albums, then you should think about just pressing singles to start out with. CD singles are always the way to test the waters. This not only saves you money, but it keeps your upcoming CD album fresh longer. You can release another single after 6-8 weeks. This will give the radio audience a chance to warm up to your product. After (2) singles become popular then consider releasing album length CDs. The large labels always release new artist singles first when testing the market.

Depending on the size of your city, 500-1000 pieces should be more than enough to start out with. You will usually have to sell about 1000 pieces to break even (make back what you have spent in pressing this product). You may have to give away "Free Copies" (not for sale or promotional copies) to industry people such as DJs, nightclub owners, large label executives, radio program directors, local newspapers and magazines. Usually, the record pressing plant will supply you with a few over-run copies free of charge. This is standard for most plants but you may want to ask to be sure.

<u>Your budget isn't large enough to tackle the world. Pursue your career in this order:</u>

1) Locally   (Your city & cities within your state),
2) Regionally (Cities within 3-4 states adjoining your state)
3) Nationally (Keep adding cities and states at a time, until you cover the whole USA)
4) Internationally   (Foreign Countries)

Color or Black & White?

Most new artists and record labels make the mistake of thinking that all of their printed items must be in full color. When first starting out, you should always go black and white, unless you have thousands of dollars to invest on the <u>printing</u> (inserts, posters, etc.). A good graphic artist can do wonders with black and white photos, artwork and / or logos. The major labels release superstar artists' products in black & white from time-to-time! If your song is hot then listeners could care less about the color of the insert when they stop into the record store to buy it. Have you ever not bought a hot single that you went into a record store to buy just because the insert was in black & white?

In recent years, duplication plants have developed a way to make color or black & white inserts (CD) for almost the same price range. The problem is that when it comes to posters the prices are very different. Color posters can cost anywhere from a few hundred dollars to thousands more than black and white posters. Be consistent with your release products. Posters should be the same color as the release inserts.

By the end of the 90s duplication houses started offering reasonable priced CD color packages. Many indie labels prior to this point were releasing Black and White product because it was a few hundred dollars cheaper. With the advancement of the home computer including powerful color scanners, digital cameras, CD label printing software and typeset programs....a lot of labels / bands are now doing <u>prepress</u> ("camera ready") color jobs at home! This will continue to lower the cost of what dup houses are charging for color jobs. Thus most indie labels today are springing for the color jobs because the public will think that the artist is "big time" when visually comparing the indie product to the major label product while shopping in record retail stores.

Finished Products

<u>The basic products that you will need to launch your new artist will be</u>:

CD Maxi-Singles
Album length CDs (Optional at this point. Test the water with singles first.)
8x10 Black & White Photos (with contact info and label logo printed on these)
Press release (artist biography, accomplishments, past shows / performances, etc.)
Posters
Magazine Ads with ordering info (Consult magazines for their film specifications)
New Release Flyers and postcards

<u>These other products containing artist's and label's name / logos can be sold at all appearances</u>:

| T-shirts | Pens/Pencils | Caps | Lyric Booklets with artist photos |
| Stickers | Cups/Mugs | Bandanas | Buttons |

Also start a website for your label to include MP3 samples of your releases and product ordering information. Include a message board where you can promote your label and artists, as well!! Your internet service provider can assist you with this.

A duplication / replication company named **Disc Makers** is very popular among independent record labels. Visit their site at: **www.discmakers.com/music**

CHAPTER 6

Getting Heard, Seen and Bought

Independent Record Distribution

Every artist and label love the idea of having their record releases in record stores everywhere. Who wouldn't? The only problem is how long can you wait for your profits to come rolling in? Is 2 - 4 months okay? How many CDs or tapes can you afford to have someone lose or swear that you've never shipped the product to them? How patient are you in dealing with companies who you've given your product to only to be given the run around every time you call to inquire about your monies due from record sells. Do you enjoy being put on hold for 10-20 minutes at a time when calling long distance?

If you can deal with these things fairly well, then you may be ready to deal with a record distributor. If not, you will be better off handling your own distribution through One-stops and record store managers on consignment. One-stops (small distributors) who sell new release product to mom's & pop's (privately owned record stores) in smaller nearby cities. Most One-stops cover service regionally (in three or more neighboring states). Actually, they cover some of the same stores that major distributors cover. The difference is that One-stops will carry more regionally indie products and distributors will carry mostly major record label products. Most distributors won't carry an independent product unless the product is already hot on the radio and is being asked for by large record chains.

I've found that indie labels have a better chance of getting paid from smaller private owned One-stops and local record stores rather than distributors. One-stops and private owned record stores can pay you right out of their cash registers as they sell your product. Distributors have to deal with submitting your paperwork to several people and offices, before actually cutting and mailing you a check. This could take months before you get paid for the sell of product. Also, that's if someone doesn't lose your paperwork between offices.

Buy some 3-part NCR invoices at your local copy shop and have the copy shop to copy your logo and contact info onto these. Why 3-parts? For each record store account that you open, you will need a copy, the stores will need a copy, and your accountant will need a copy. Consignment agreements can range from 30 - 90 days. Placing product **on consignment** simply means that they will stock your product for the consignment period that is agreed upon and pay you for what they have sold when this period is up (30 - 90 days later).Placing your product with a One-stop and local record store owners is easy. You simply get in touch with the purchasing departments (One-Stops) or the store managers (Local record stores). Let these people know that you are a new indie label with a new artist release that you'd like to place in their store (or stores) on consignment. Then simply make an appointment to take or mail your product to their store (or stores) and have your invoice signed by whomever receives it.

You will need to have them sign your 3-part consignment invoice for the amount of product that you will be leaving them. Try to negotiate for the shortest amount of days and give them only 5-peices or less of your product. Stores only put out a small quantity of CDs or cassettes for customers, don't give stores more product than they can put on their shelves. It can sometimes be a pain for them to find storage space for your extra copies. Be sure to leave your business card so that they can contact you if they need to re-order. If your product becomes in demand you can then ask for cash upon delivery. By then, most of these stores will be glad to pay you up front just to have your product in their stores.

When placing your product on consignment, keep in mind that you are charging these retail outlets (One-stops & record stores) wholesale prices, not the price that their customers pay. It's customary for the new record label to get paid 40%-50% of the money that the product retails for. The record store profits 50%-60% of what the product retails for.

<u>The going wholesale rates that independent labels make are:</u>

$7.50 - $10.75 per album CD sold
$4.00 - $5.00 for each CD maxi-single sold

<u>When you assign your products to a record retailer using your consignment invoices you will list</u>:

Today's Date and Length of the consignment
Quantity (How many)
The Product Title (Name of the song or album, and the artist's name)
The Recorded Medium (CD, CD single, album length cassette, cassette maxi-single, or vinyl)
The Record Number (From the bar code for easy logging and tracking via computer)
How much you are charging the retailer per piece (wholesale price the label wants to make)
Total of how much the retailer will owe you if he sells all of the product on this consignment

EXAMPLE:

"Cool Song Man" by: Artist's NAME
(5) album length CDs /record number: UGR12004
at $7.50 each
Amount Due $37.50
Net in 30-Days
STORE OWNER'S SIGNATURE

At the end of your consignment period, contact all stores that are due and find out how many copies they have sold. Close the old consignments and collect for sold product. If the store would still like to carry your product have them sign a new consignment agreement for the unsold product. Or if the product is in demand have them pay you up front for the re-order!
*Always leave a few posters, a 8x10 B&W Photo with text, and a demo CD at each retail outlet to help the store promote your products.

The best way to <u>recoup</u> (Make back your money) and to make a profit is to sell your own tapes and CDs at your shows. Sell your product at shows and pocket 98% of what it will cost in stores instead of the 40%-50% that you will be getting from retail store owners.

College Radio

For new indie labels chances of receiving radio air play are better with a college radio station. These stations have student DJs for almost every format of music at various times of the day or on various nights. Again, contact the station's Program Director or Music Director for names and addresses to send your press release to.

College radio stations will play your single and also do on-air interviews for your artist. They can also assist you with setting up an engagement for your artist on their campus! Remember that your artist will need a <u>following</u> (Fans who love to see the artist perform and will buy the artist recordings). On a college campus, there are people from many different cities, also other countries, who will spread the word about your artist. These students will buy your products right on the spot when the artist gives a performance on the college campus.

Industry magazines such as **Gavin Report**, and **CMJ**; monitor college radio stations' airplay and will review new independent artists and /or record labels in their magazines articles. Major label executives read these magazines and listen to college radio stations for new talent to sign.

Local Radio Stations

* Local Radio: Non-college Commercial Radio stations in cities across the US that play Top 100, Top 40 and New Releases in formats such as Pop, Urban/Hip-Hop, R&B, Country,..etc.

Since radio stations only play singles, I don't understand why new indie labels waste money attempting to release album length product. There is no guaranty in this business that you will have a hit on your first release. So, why not release CD maxi-singles (1-5 songs on a CD)? Use the rest of your budget for advertising and promotions. Your first objective should be to create a name within the industry for your label and a following for your artist.

Don't go into this business with high hopes of getting rich the first time around. This business is a gamble just like any other business. If you can't accept failure, then you are in the wrong business!

In order for your single to receive <u>radio air play</u> (be put into rotation or on a play list to be heard a certain number of times per day), it must first be approved by the radio station's <u>Program Director</u> (PD) or <u>Music Director</u> (MD). Contact the radio stations who play your format of music, get names and addresses. Mail your press release packages to these stations' PDs. Most radio stations, nightclubs and retail record outlets' customer listening stations play only CDs, so order a few CDs for promotional or give-away purposes.

<u>Local Radio stations will usually give your single a spin if some of these things are happening</u>:

-The artist is already performing around town regularly and has a large following

-If the single has <u>distribution</u> (is it in retail record outlets) so that listeners can buy it

-The single fits the station's format and there are many listener requests

-Your label is willing to give away product to the station's listeners while conducting an "On-air artist interview"

-Your label or it's artist is sponsoring a city-wide benefit that is creating a lot of
  attention for a good cause

-Your label is spending bucks for advertising spots on the radio like the major labels
(Advertising rates range from $95.00 and up for (1) 30-second spot on major city radio stations)

Small Town Radio

Small town radio stations have inexpensive advertising rates for promoting your single. They are also always looking for a new artist from the local region (2-4 state area) to put into their rotation. These Program Directors are usually down to earth. Contact stations in nearby small cities who play your format of music. Visit these stations in a professional manner, buy ad spots and they will play your single. Ask for on-air interviews for your artist and **product give-aways** for listeners who call in to request to hear your product. These radio stations will be glad to be the first station in their area to have had contact with your label and /or artist. Also, they can help you with information on setting up a show for your artist in their city. This will be great for artist exposure and product sells!

These smaller station PDs also know PDs of stations in other larger cities and can put in a good word to......perhaps the local station in your city, if you have a potential hit. They can also put out bad info about you if you or your artists aren't conducting yourselves professionally.

To stay current with programming all PDs attend radio programming trade shows as well as read radio programming magazines. Therefore, it's not uncommon for PDs across many states to know each other personally.

The Press

There are several forms of press that a new label will need to effectively promote an artist. As a new label you should contact and send artist press release kits to any of the below whose readers would buy your label's type of music.

Local Music Papers/ fanzines
Local Daily Newspapers
Local Ethnic Newspapers
College Newspapers
High School Newspapers
Consumer Magazines
Music Trade Magazines

Local Music Papers (or fanzines) are usually for free and found laying around in record stores, musical instrument stores and major bookstores. These magazines contain information such as: artists' nightclub show dates, this week's or this month's top hits in various genres of music (Formats or types of music), new release reviews, superstars and new artists articles, concert dates and reviews, etc.

Local Daily Newspapers are home delivered each morning to subscribers in and around your city's surrounding county areas (very large distribution). These newspapers have entertainment writers/reporters who cover and write articles about: bands, recording artists, movies, dining, actors/actresses, plays, comedians and so on. Local newspapers will have a daily page dedicated to entertainment, as well as a weekend insert booklet with new record releases and movie ads.

Local Ethnic Newspaper (Latino American, Chinese American, African American, etc.) are found in major metropolitan areas (medium to large cities) and are targeted toward interests of a particular race of people. These newspapers also contain record reviews and articles about new artists. You would use this newspaper to promote your artist to a particular audience of people.

College Newspapers are found on college campuses and have student reporters who would love to cover new record labels, review new artists and their recordings, as well as attend and review your performance on their campus!!! You are almost guaranteed local college radio airplay and good free promotion for your artists if you give a good show on their campus.

High School Newspapers can be found at most modern large high schools. These high schools also may have student radio/cable TV programming. This is a very good market for a local indie label /artist to win!!!

Consumer Music Magazines appeal to people who buy and listen to mostly one type of music (Rock, Dance, Modern Rock, New World, R&B / Hip-Hop, Country, Classical, Jazz, etc..). These magazines will have: ads of recording artists' new releases/reviews, clothing and perfume ads from brand name fashion designers, articles about what's going on with a certain band or artist, music charts, movie ads and reviews. This magazine has subscribers all over the world. A review of your artist/label in this magazine would reach the masses. To advertise in this magazine is very expensive, but effective.

Trade Magazines (Recording Industry / Music Business news magazines) are read by professional industry people such as:

Record label executives, record distributors and store owners, radio station PDs, nightclub owners and talent buyers, music publishers and professional songwriters, some TV and Movie industry executives (movie producers also use recordings for soundtracks), artist management companies, etc.

These people stay on top of such weekly or daily things such as:

-How well their artist is doing on the charts
-Other record releases that are becoming hits in a particular style of music
-What recordings are being sold, how fast and by what type of buyer...
   ...(ie..teens, women, etc.)
-What changes are going on in the industry and the latest business trends
-Who's currently in the studio working on new recordings (Producer/artist/label)
-Who wrote, published, or produced a certain song

...........and other recording industry related information.
(Refer to Chapter 2- "Staying Current and Knowing Your Trade" and Chapter 4- "Setting A Release Date")

Nightclubs

If your artist isn't a <u>minor</u> (a child who's under your state's legal drinking or contractual agreement age) it would be to your benefit for your artist to perform in nightclubs to boost product (new release CD) sells and to create a following for your artist. Most nightclubs are open to local artists who have new record releases. The main concern of the club owner is whether or not he can make a profit by letting you perform in his club?

Upon releasing your new artist single you should rent a nightclub for a <u>Release Party</u> (a party where local music industry people are invited to check out your new artist and your label's staff). Invite local industry people such as Radio Station Program Directors, Record store owners, music fanzine and newspaper's entertainment reporters, nightclub owners, and of course the general public who likes your artist's genre (type of music). The admission, food and drink for the industry people should be complimentary. The general public should be charged an admission price which will include the artist's performance, a free CD, and <u>refreshments</u> (food and drinks). By doing this you will not only be creating a professional image in the eyes of the industry people, but your artist will also be creating a <u>following</u> (loyal fans that will come to every show) and you will be making some of your money back....and hopefully a large profit (all in the same night)!

Another way to build a following for your artist is to have your artist to open for major acts who are on a nightclub tour. If these crowds accept your artist, then afterwards your label will start receiving calls from local record stores (the ones that you have sent press releases to a month ago) for product. Also, it'll be easy to get booked in other clubs in cities throughout your region. Radio stations will start giving your product airplay....especially if these program directors were in the crowd! If you are lucky one of the major label executives, who will be at this major artist show, will approach you for <u>a deal</u> (a $$$$$$ agreement) with your artist and/or label!

If a major artist's management likes your artist, then he might want to also negotiate a deal with your label involving your artist to continue the rest of the major artist tour as the "*opening act*". This will make your label a lot of money quickly....but, remember to let your entertainment attorney advise and negotiate all of your contracts for you.

Television Commercials

Small Indie labels usually don't have the budget to run television commercials. These commercials can range anywhere from $500.00 and up per 30-second spot for a commercial during prime time. Not to mention the expense of a video cameraman to shoot this footage for your artist. However, if your advertising budget allows this, you will be able to reach a large number of people with one shot.

The key to effective TV commercials is knowing your audience's favorite TV shows. For example, if you were advertising to kids (say 8 to 13-years old) then you would run your ads during cartoon programming, say after school or Saturday mornings. It wouldn't make much sense to run your commercials during school hours, between soap operas.

Your local TV station sales reps can assist you in effective commercial times and days for the audience that you are trying to reach. TV stations have information of viewers for every hour of the day (such as age group, race and gender). Arrange to meet with one of these TV reps if you are consider running commercials on TV.

The best time to run a TV commercial is when your artist is getting ready to do a show, have press coverage, have radio air play and have products in local record stores. MENTION THESE THINGS IN YOUR COMMERCIAL!!!!!!! Don't waste this time with info that your artist has released a song, so have thousands of other unknown artists.

Music Videos

Let us determine if your small <u>indie</u> (Independent) label needs a music video for their first new artist release....Hmmm.....

-*Do you know the requirements for submitting your video to MTV, BET, VHS-1, or any other music video station? Have you contacted these people for info? This info can be found in Billboard Magazine.*

-*Do you have another minimum of $10,000 to invest after paying for your new artist's CDs?*

-*Are you selling hundreds of CDs & Tapes from local retail outlets?*

-*Does your artist have shows booked in major cities across 5-6 states in the next month or so?*

-*Is your artists getting good press coverage in regional newspapers, music magazines, and record store chain magazines?*

-*Is your artist getting reviews in industry magazines like Billboard?*

-*Does your budget allow you to supply all the record stores in say a 500 mile radius with hundreds of CDs or tapes overnight?*

-*Is your artist in the Top 10 play list on regional radio stations (3-4 state area including your city)?*

-*Is your label getting calls from industry people wanting to negotiate deals with you for your artist?*

If the answer to most of these is NO, ...then you may not be ready yet to produce a music video for your artist.

*Of course this might be debatable if you know someone personally who owns video equipment and will make the video for a small fee just to help you out. Or if your town has a local independent or small cable TV station that air local bands' music videos.

Chapter 7

Welcome To The Recording Industry

You have made it to the final chapter. I've exposed to the realities of starting your own independent record label. For some this business can be rewarding and for some headaches as well as bankruptcy. The key to making it in this business is somewhat like the Boy Scout Motto....BE PREPARED.

For a quick review......

<u>You will be required to read in this business therefore:</u>

-Study your business by buying and reading the books I've outlined for you in Chapter 2. Build your reference library continuously with current editions of these and other books that come along.

-Learn to read, understand, and to negotiate the industry agreements (Contracts) that you will be using or that you will be offered. ALWAYS LET YOUR ENTERTAINMENT ATTORNEY ADVISE AND NEGOTIATE THESE FOR YOU.

-Read trade magazines weekly so you will know what's going on.

Build this group of business associates for your label:

Banker
(Meet a loan officer when you open your business checking account.)

Entertainment Attorney
(This person will protect you from getting ripped off or sued.)

Certified Public Accountant
(Will help you to pay your bills, royalties, IRS, and account for all of your expenses for your label's business deductions / returns. Save all receipts, cancelled checks, company checking deposit/withdrawal slips to this person)

Graphics Artist / Layout Person
(Let this person do all of your artwork and logos. Everything from business cards to CD inserts, Posters, and "Thank You" postcards.)

Commercial Printer
(Use this guy, unless you want your products looking like they were done on a portable office copier.)

Pressing Plant
(These plants also do CD replication / Audio Cassette Duplication and packaging your inserts that your printer will send them.)

Recording Studio & Engineer
(If your producer / arranger doesn't own his own.)

Commercial Photographer
(Experienced in photographing models and entertainers)

Radio Station Program Directors
(Build a file of stations who play your music format. Always send thank you calls or cards to a PD who puts your record into airplay rotation or play lists. These people can spread the word to other stations about how professional your organization is or how popular your product is becoming.) **Radio & Record Magazine has a list of stations' play lists (all genres) and addresses. A label exec will read this magazine to see which stations have added his label's new single to their play lists.**

Local Record Store Owners

Some of these owners will own chains or service other cities as a One-Stop for your region. They will also know other chain owners and One Stops in regions that they don't service. These owners can spread the word to major record company reps about your product, because they come in contact with industry people regularly. Record stores also report record activity to trade magazines so that the whole industry will know about your hit and where to place it on the Top 40 or Top 100 Charts.

Keep these people informed of your radio airplay, club dates and appearances by either a call or a professional post card which should have your label logo on it. When you decide to go regional with your product let these owners know and maybe you can get distribution through them or one of their business associates in other cities. Always send thanks to these people and be patient for their payments for your consignment product. If you call to inquire about a past due consignment don't get upset if they can't talk to you at that moment. Ask when would be a good time to call again, understand that they are busy, and wish them a nice day. You might check you mailbox the next day an find a check along with a re-order request.

Local and Regional Nightclub Owners - These guys are always interested in new artists who are drawing crowds. If you already have radio airplay and have independent record distribution, then you should be performing to promote your product. You can set-up tables to sell your CDs, tapes, T-shirts, etc..from and make a nice profit at each performance. Also the club go-ers will believe that you are an artist and will support you by buying your product (If your artist performs well). If your first club appearance is a success then you won't have trouble getting booked at other clubs that play your format of music. Nightclubs will prepare your artist for larger concert halls and coliseum. Once your label becomes known to the nightclub owners, every new artist that your label releases will be welcome to perform in their clubs. Build a file of these people.

Local Press - Read local music newspapers, college newspapers, and local daily newspapers to find names of entertainment reporters who review new recordings and who write articles on local new artists. Contact these people by calling their paper and request an address to send you artist's press release kit to. These people can put you in contact with the press reporters in other cities when you are ready to go regional.

Locally Then Regionally

You are not a major label yet so don't attempt to <u>conquer the world</u> (to go national) with your first release. As a new indie label you should focus more on building an audience following for your artist locally, then regionally. A regional hit can make you rich, as well as attract major labels to you offering BIG MONEY deals for your artist! The major labels will find you if you are successful. Major labels have talent scouts who go to all major cities and some country towns looking for talent. These scouts not only monitor the radio stations they come to local artists' shows. Especially if that local artist has a following, radio requests, and is performing regularly regionally.

Concentrate on booking more shows, doing radio interviews / give-aways, and setting up <u>retail outlet appearances</u> (autographed "For copies purchased" signing sessions) for your artist. These things should allow your label to <u>recoup</u> (make back) most of the money that you have invested in releasing your artist, to be able to pay royalties, and to see a profit for your label. A radio commercial would be very beneficial if your artist is doing a show. Along with the show information, mention things like where to buy the product and what the press or magazines reviewers are saying about your artist...and your new label.

Use your advertising budget mostly for industry and consumer magazine ads. Your second goal should be to try to make your money back and hopefully a profit. If you only break even, then you have achieved something that most new indie labels don't on their first release.

Try to attract the major labels' attention to your artist by arranging for your artists to perform at industry showcases. Also, contact major tour companies or talent agencies to offer your artist as an opening act for a major artist who is planning to tour through your city. Opening for a major act in your own town would be great for local and regional record sales!

If your label has been doing it's homework and your artist already has a following, then getting your artist booked as an opening act might be easier than you think! These agencies might have already heard about your artist through one of their <u>local talent scouts </u>(the guy in the dark corner at each of your artist sold-out club gigs)!

Paying Your Artist, Songwriter & Producer

Year after year, I read about record label <u>disputes</u> (law suits and sometimes violence) involving artists, songwriters and/or producers that feel that they haven't been compensated properly by their record label. Also, from time to time, there are stories about labels that go bankrupt after having a few hit singles, because of poor accounting which results in their spending the profits before paying royalties.

It is very important to deposit all monies from record store sales into the record label's bank account. Your accountant should be given all check stubs and bank deposit receipts from these sales. Do not spend any of this money until you have paid the label's expenses and fulfilled your contractual royalty obligations to the <u>other parties </u>who are involved in your release projects (your artist, songwriter (s) and producer).

Remember the artist receives royalties only after the label has recouped expenses!

<u>This is an example of how **Mechanical royalties** can be calculated, subtracted and paid from retail sells</u>:

CD Retail Price		$17.95
Minus Retail Outlet's Percentage	40%	$ 7.18
Label Receives	60%	$10.77
Minus Label's Expenses on packaging	10%	$ 1.08
Label's Net		$ 9.69
Producer (s) Royalty 3% of Net		.29 (divided among the number of producers)
Publisher's & Songwriter's Mechanical Royalty		.80 (.08-cents per song for a 10-song CD)
Artist's Royalty 8% of Net		.77
Label's Profit		$7.83

Artist royalties are usually paid every 6-months after recoupment of monies spent. Read more about this in a copy of **"This Business Of Music"**.

<u>Your accountant will be able to total the amount of all royalties due to the label, as well as to all of your people by the percentage that each one agreed upon within the following agreements:</u>

Record Label / Recording Artist Agreement - (Usually the artist will be paid royalties after certain label expenses have been made back (Recouped).

The Publisher / Songwriter Agreement - (for your songwriter (s))

The Record Label / Producer Agreement - (for your producer)

Note: *If your producer is also the artist (artist/songwriter/arranger & producer) he will receive royalties from all three of the above agreements.*

<u>How often everyone will receive royalties</u> (Royalty Payment Periods) is written in the above agreements. Most indie labels and publishers pay <u>bi-annually</u> (every 6-months) in the form of checks. Performance Rights Organizations pay royalty checks directly to its publishers and songwriters <u>quarterly</u> (every 4-months).

Also, your accountant will be able to withhold and pay taxes for the label and the other parties involved. Therefore, the accountant will prepare royalty statements to accompany all royalty checks. Keeping you out of trouble with the IRS is also part of your accountant's job.

With the understanding of agreements and accounting, everyone will profit whenever there is a good selling product. A happy label is a strong label, because everyone will enjoy his role and work hard. Everything becomes be fun and the parties who are involved will become more like a family.

See "This Business Of Music" and "The Musicians Business and Legal Guide", for an in-depth study of various agreements and royalty payment periods.

GO FOR IT!!!!!!!!!!!!!!!!

Chapter 8

Selling and Promoting on the Internet

Start a website for your label to include MP3 samples of your releases and product ordering information. Include a message board where you can promote your label and artists, as well!! Your internet service provider can assist you with this.

There are many independent recording artists who are selling CDs as well as MP3 downloads of their songs over the internet without the help of a distributor. People are also actually buying MP3 downloads to play in their MP3 walkmans and/or MP3 CD car stereo systems!

This can be done through several online music companies. These companies can design the artist a web page (with a link to his/her custom web site with purchase options) where people form all over the world can listen to and buy a new independent artist's CDs as well as the artist's other merchandise online with a credit card!

Some of the most well know online companies are: **MP3.com**, **CDbaby.com** and **CDStreet.com**. On the artist's custom web site (*your service internet provider can assist you with designing and managing this*) a new artist (unsigned / undiscovered) can not only upload MP3 samples of his/her CD for the world to listen to and purchase, but also post and update band/artist information (tour/ appearance dates/ bios/ photos), manage a message board and receive response forms for fans. Sell your Mp3 downloads at **Liquidaudio.com** for a fee.

Some of these companies charge a small one time fee of about $50.00 for their services, which is well worth the money. They will keep some of your CDs in inventory, make your web page from the info and photos, also make MP3 samples for people to listen to from the finished promotional CD that you send them. They will also process online orders for you! Some of these companies can even process the sale of MP3 downloads for you. Visit the above companies online for more information.

Emailing MP3s and Burning Audio CDs

To create an MP3 of your music you must first record your master recordings from a CD or DAT to a computer. This can be done by plugging your CD or DAT player into your computer's sound card audio inputs with a stereo RCA cable and using audio recording software. Next you will need to process your music files...ie..EQ, noise removal or hiss, normalize the volume levels, then trim it to the correct length in order to create samples for uploads and/or emails.. Software such as **MusicMatch Jukebox**, **Cool Edit**, and **RealJukebox** are great for this! Also with this software you can also burn audio CDs for demos that will play in home and car stereo systems. Another good software program for burning audio CDs from MP3 files (..and printing custom labels for your CDs) is **Burn & Go** which can be found at computer, software and most large electronics department stores.

With the proper MP3 software you can also email samples of your MP3s to fans, industry contacts (with their permission, of course!) and friends. Keep in mind when emailing an MP3 file you only want to email a few seconds of the sample, because a full 3-4 minute song would take the receiver a few hours to download and can crash some computer systems! **MSN Messenger Service** can assist you with this.

Here are a few good books on this subject:

Publishing Music Online by Paul Sellars
The Musician's Guide To The Internet by Rodd Souvignier and Gary Hustwit
How To Promote Your Music Successfully On The Internet by Midnight Rain Productions
The Indie Bible by David Wimble
The MP3 and Internet Audio Handbook by Bruce Fries with Marty Fries

Free useful online information e-zines & newsletters to subscribe to:

Galaris.com
thebuzzfactor.com
Indie-Music.com
MusicMorsels.com
Artistpro.com
MusesMuse.com

Other New Artist Music Related Internet Information:

Iuma.com
SonicNet.com
SunsetRadio.com

APPENDIX 1

INFORMATION SOURCES

Library Of Congress
Copyright Office
101 Independence Avenue, S.E.
Washington, DC 20559-6000
(202) 707-9100
http://lcweb.loc.gov/copyright

Uniform Code Council, Inc.
7887 Washington Village Drive, Suite 300
Dayton, OH 45459
(937) 435-3870
http://www.uc-council.org

ASCAP
American Society Of Composers, Authors, And Publishers
One Lincoln Plaza
New York, NY 10023
(212) 595-3050
http://www.ascap.com

BMI
Broadcast Music Incorporated
320 West 57th Street
New York, NY 10019
(212) 586-2000
http://www.bmi.com

SESAC
10 Columbus Circle
New York, NY 10019
(212) 586-3450
http://www.sesac.com

Local Industry People Check List
You Have Ordered PA, SR, and CA copyright forms along with the Copyright Basics Booklet!

YOU ARE NOT READY TO START YOUR LABEL UNTIL YOU HAVE THE BELOW LIST FILLED OUT.

Bank:_____

Entertainment Attorney:_____

Accountant (CPA):_____

Commercial Photographer:_____

Graphic Artist:_____

Commercial Printer:_____

Pressing Plant:_____

Recording Studio:_____

Recording Engineer:_____

Nightclub /Owners: _____

_____

_____

Record Store Chain / Owners:_____

_____

_____

Radio Station / PD: _____

_____

Entertainment Reporters/Writers:

Daily Newspaper: _____

Music Fanzine: _____

College Newspaper: _____

_____

Public Library: _____

Book Store: _____

(Meet with all the above people. Remember to record names and phone numbers)

APPENDIX 3

OTHER 411

The Musician's Atlas - Has a listing (with contact information)of all College & Local radio stations across the USA by format (genre). Also included is contact info for entertainment attorneys, A&R people and record labels, nightclubs and venues, record retailers and distributors, fanzines and local newspapers, dup houses, booking agents, studios, promo companies, custom merchandising companies, website designers, etc.....very informative for a new label!!! This book sells for about $25.00 at your local retail book chain. BUY IT!!!!

The Musician's Guide To Touring and Promotion - This book contains some of the information that The Musician's Atlas does and is also good information for a new label. Certain yearly editions of this book will contain a list of major talent showcases across the USA. Costs between $9-$15 at your local retail book chain.

Pollstar.com - This site will list the amounts of money that concerts are grossing by artist, as well as other industry touring information!

Showcase Your Artist

Most cities have local or regional talent shows which are attended by industry talent scouts (people who are searching for new artists to sign to their record label). These people are always looking for the next big star. If your artist can move the audience and is selling lots of Cds locally, then chances are this person will want to talk to your label.

Your label's participation in industry talent showcases will be observed and noted by all industry people. This not only shows professionalism on your part, but it will also help with your radio acceptance, boost your record sales, and/or attract major labels who might want to offer you big money deals for the worldwide distribution of your artist. ***The following magazines have annual industry showcases that indie labels as well as major labels participate in:**

Magazine Name:	Format:
CMJ	Alternative, Rock &Roll
Radio and Record	All
Billboard	All
Urban Network	R&B/Black/Rap
Black Radio and Entertainment (BRE)	R&B/Black/Rap
Jack The Rapper	R&B/Black/Rap

*Phone these magazines for their showcase information and dates. Call your local library for these phone numbers!

APPENDIX 4 iv

A SAMPLE CONSIGNMENT FORM

-INVOICE NUMBER-

YOUR RECORD COMPANY'S LOGO
USED GEAR RECORDS
P.O. BOX 15678
MEMPHIS, TN 38518
(901) 830-0910

ARTIST: WAREHOUSEMEN
SELECTION: MACHINE ANIMAL
MEDIA: CD ALBUM
RECORD NUMBER: UGR10978
BARCODE: YES

QUANTITY   20 CDs at $10.77@
AMOUNT DUE $215.40

USED GEAR RECORDS REP: _____

STORE MANAGER'S SIGNATURE:_____

DATE: /   /

BALANCE DUE IN 30-DAYS or UPON SALE OF PRODUCT

Please Note: A new consignment agreement must be negotiated after 30-days and at this time all monies from product sold will be due.

Trademark

Before applying for a trademark you must:

-Secure Business License
-Do a name search
-File a "use" or a "intent to use"Application along with fee and mark (Artwork).

*Obtain federal Trademark by using your record distribution list as proof that you have crossed state lines (Product in various stores in other states).

*File a "Use" application if mark has already been used by person filing.
*Conduct a search by:

       contacting......

       General Information Services Division
       U.S. Patent and Trademark Office
       Crystal Plaza 3, Room 2C02
       Washington, DC 20231

Phone: (800) 786-9199
Web Address: **http://www.uspto.gov**

-If you have already started to a mark commercially then file the "use" Application and Fee (currently approx. $325.00) along with a Black & White drawing of the mark (onced registered drawing can be used in whatever color you desire).

-If you haven't used the mark yet in commerce then you will file the "intent to use" application and fee which is $475.00 ($150.00 + $325.00) along with your Black & White mark.

*Use circle R beside your logo on all products afterwards.

*Valid for a period of 10-years.

*Must file affidavit between the 5th & 6th year to keep Trademark alive.

TAXATION CONSIDERATIONS

****KEEP ALL RECEIPTS AND CANCELLED CHECKS IN ONE ENVELOPE****

*Your Label must generate income totaling more than debt of below within your 3rd year in business to avoid a "Hobby Status" with IRS. Request info from the Internal Revenue Service concerning "Hobby Status". If your label falls into this status IRS could charge you serious back taxes.

Office Rental
Insurance
Utilities
Office Supplies
Business Machine Rental
Club/Venue Rental
Musical Equipment Rental

You must serve a "Miscellaneous Income Form 1099" at the end of the year to independent contractors below in which Label paid more than $600.00 to within the tax year. Label is also required to submit a copy to IRS.

(Set up tax with-holding % info for states label will be making a profit in. Check list of deduction codes.)

Entertainment Attorney's Fees
Consultant Fees
Midi Programmer/Musical Arranger Fees
Studio Rental (Engineer fee &Tapes)
Session Players
Stage Equipment Rental (And Sound and Light People)
Trademark Registration and Search Fees

Allowable Travel, Entertainment, and other Misc. Expenses:

Hotel and Truck Rental for a performance
Music Conferences, Industry Seminars, and Classes
Planned Business Meals with Industry Persons
Trade Magazine Subscriptions
Performance Rights Organization Fees and Union Dues
Promotional Expenses: (Postage, Phone Bills, Photo copying, faxing, overnight mail delivery fees)
Photo Costs
Equipment Insurance costs
Automobile Expenses

**   Get more tax information on the web at: http://www.irs.gov   **

Check List For Starting Up A Record Label Business

_____ 1) Filing DBA / Business License with your county clerks' office.

_____ 2) Resale License.

_____ 3) Tax Number from your state's Department of Revenue

_____ 4) Checking account For Publishing wing and Checking account for Label.

_____ 5) Trademark Search and Registration.

_____ 6) Performance Rights Affiliation as Publisher Member.

_____ 7) PA, CA and SR copyrights forms.

_____ 8) UPC Registration (Bar Code)

_____ 9) <u>Attorney to draft the following contracts for the Record Label</u>:
   (*Also have him to explain these to you in plain English)

        Songwriter/Publisher Contracts
        Recording Artist Contracts
        Record Production Contracts
        Mechanical License
        Artist Production Contracts
        Artist Management Agreement
        Musician Release Forms
        Background Singers Release Forms
        Model Release Forms
        Actors/Actress Release Forms
        Work-For-Hire Forms
        Photo Release Form
        Graphic Artists/Design Agreements
        Studio "Spec" Agreements
        Promotion Agreements
        Agent Agreements
        Artist/Staff Agreements
        Lawyer/Engagement Agreements

Demos and Releases

Unless you want your release to sound like it was recorded on someone's cheap cassette recorder, you should use professional musical and recording equipment. All major and the successful indie labels use professional equipment on all of their hit releases. If you can't afford this equipment then you can usually find this in recording studios.... for use during recording sessions only. Some large music stores rent professional equipment on a daily basis.

If you or your producer do not know about midi musical and digital recording equipment then educate yourself. Go to local music stores for workshops and demonstrations. Make sure to learn about samplers. Listen to radio and CDs you like and try to match sounds to equipment that you've heard in music stores. Order info packages from companies who make this equipment.

Here are a list of some well known companies who make the professional equipment that hit cds are recorded with:

Roland	**Tascam**	**Yamaha**
Ensoniq	**Mackie**	**Korg**
Kurzweil	**Alesis**	**Akai**
Emu	**Shure**	

That Major Label Sound

IMPORTANT!!!!!!....You will want to have your masters brought up to broadcast quality by having it mastered by a professional mastering engineer. This engineer will use equalizers, effects and massive amounts of compression to skillfully make your CD sound as loud and clean as the major labels releases! A mastering engineer can be found in major recording studios in most cities. Industry professional and A&R people can hear the difference between a professionally mastered demo and a non-professionally produced demo!

INDEX